A

A Seaside Alphabet

B

TEXT BY DONNA GRASSBY
ART BY SUSAN TOOKE

TUNDRA BOOKS

C

A SEASIDE ALPHABET

I love to be by the sea! Come with me and leap with delight over smooth granite rocks at Peggy's Cove. Heed the mournful lament of a foghorn near Wood Islands. Savor the taste of a lobster boil on Old Orchard Beach. Whiff the crisp, salt sea air where humpback whales breach in Notre Dame Bay. Time the tides and witness a waterfall stop and reverse its direction near Saint John.

A seaside adventure can be exhilarating, and when you come prepared, you may discover timeless treasures. Before you explore *A Seaside Alphabet*, let me share background information to guide you on the journey.

Everywhere that ocean meets land is called coast. Coastlines are altered continually by currents, winds, and tides that ceaselessly batter islands, beaches, cliffs, and marshes. While some areas near the seaside appear bleak and windblown, they may be teeming with life.

Tides in the Bay of Fundy are the highest in the world. When the tide goes out, the exposed mudflats come alive with worms, clams, small crustaceans, snails, and mussels. These creatures attract and nourish thousands of waterfowl and shorebirds during their long migration from Canada's Arctic. The return of the tide replenishes the mudflats, making them vital feeding grounds.

Coastal waters are dotted with islands, many of which have fascinating stories to tell. Sable Island, Nova Scotia is known as the "Graveyard of the Atlantic" because of the many shipwrecks off its shores. Funk Island, Newfoundland and Percé Rock at the head of the Gaspé Peninsula are inhabited only by seabirds. Treasure islands – like Jewell Island, Maine and Oak Island, Nova Scotia – enchant us with secret legends. Cadillac Mountain, on Mount Desert Island, Maine is one of the highest points along the Atlantic coast.

Bordering the continent of North America, a shallow submarine plain called the continental shelf extends out under the ocean for about 200 kilometers, or 125 miles. The shallow waters over the shelf allow sunlight to filter through to the ocean floor. The action of currents, winds, and tides makes this an ideal environment for sea life to thrive. While some fish stocks have been depleted, strict regulations are being enforced to protect the fragile remains of the fishing industry.

The weather along the coast is unpredictable, changeable, and relatively mild due to the moderating effect of the sea. A maritime summer may be a series of sunny days, or weeks of fog and rain. Often, it's noon before you know the kind of day it's going to be. The unpredictable nature of weather can produce sudden changes: squalls can boil up in seconds. Sailors and fishermen know the danger of being lost at sea during unforeseen storms.

Many of my friends and family rely on the sea for their livelihood, transportation, and recreation. Like the ever-changing seascape, they have been forced to adapt to unforeseen challenges, such as the decline of the traditional industries of fishing, boat-building, coal mining, and steelmaking. Even though the outlook may sometimes appear bleak, they seldom lose heart. Other opportunities are constantly being developed, including drilling for oil and natural gas, and farming mussels and oysters. In fact, the fastest growing industry along the Atlantic seaboard is the tourist trade.

My ancestors came from the Highlands of Scotland, but many other coastal residents are descended from the French, English, Irish, Welsh, Europeans, Asians, and others. Stories have been told how the Mi'kmaq welcomed early settlers by teaching them skills to survive the cold, snowy winters. Like the Mi'kmaq long ago, the maritimers' warmth, hospitality, and friendship can kindle a comfortable, secure feeling of "coming home," even to strangers.

So, come as you are to our coastal home. Susan Tooke's exquisite paintings are of real places and people who welcome the opportunity to share the treasures of the seaside with you.

Donna Grassby

Avid anglers, Angus and Anna, anchor on the arm.

B Balmy breezes blow *Bluenose II* by Boston. b

Colorful Cape Islanders come back to coastal coves with their catch.

D   Delightful dolphins dance across dark waters.   d

E   Eileen eyes elegant eagles in Englishtown.   e

F | Friends, Fergus and Fred, find Fundy fossils and "flowerpots" for fun. | f

G   Anne of Green Gables gained glory beside gentle shore grasses.   g

H   Happy humpbacks heave hefty heads high into the heavens.   h

I   Imposing icebergs idle in inlets.   i

J   Just back from jigging, Jigger Jack spies jellyfish by the jetty.   j

K   Keen Kejimkujik kayakers sight belted kingfishers.   k

L   Lovely ladies lunch on lobster in the lee of the lighthouse.   l

M   Musquodoboit mariners steam mussels in the mist.   m

N   The navy navigates The "nasty" Narrows by night.   n

Otto observes ocean caves called ovens.

P   Perky puffins prosper in perilous places.   p

 Q

Quiet craft queue in Passamaquoddy Bay.

q

R   Upriver rafters get ready to ride runaway rapids.   r

Sailors salute Cape Spear's salient shores.

T   *Titanic* treasures tossed in by the tides thrill tourists.   t

U | An unruly undertow upends Ursula. | u

V   Valiant Vikings voyaged to Vinland.   V

 Wetland wildlife watch and wade near wildflowers. W

X | Exuberant Xavier excavates for Captain Kidd's buried "X" treasure. | X

Y   Yesterday Yankee yachts raced off Yarmouth.   y

Zealous windsurfers zigzag on zephyrs.

Here is a list of what we know is in each painting. See how many you can find:

Aa   animal, auburn, apples, asters, acorns, arm, ankle, algae, L'Acadie, mountain ash

Bb   bobstay, bowsprit, booms, bear, bank, bench, back, belfry or bell tower, block, bow, backstay, black, blue

Cc   cat, captain, compass, clam, crew, coast, chain, clouds, clover, clapboard

Dd   dandelions, day, Delphinidae (toothed dolphin), dive, dorsal fin, doll, driftwood, dozen

Ee   eyes, edge, earth, ewe, ears, electrical wires, evergreens, eggs, ebony

Ff   fog, fiddler, flounder, footprints, ferns, frond, frog, feather, fir trees, fly (damsel)

Gg   galley, Glace Bay, gully, ground, Gaelic (Gàidhlig), Glooscap (in the clouds), goldenrod, gull, green

Hh   habitat, head, herring gull, haze, horizon

Ii   islands, ice, inlet, iris, iceberg

Jj   jute, jigger, jet, jut, blue jay, jackknife, Joe Batt's Arm

Kk   knots (on wood), key, kid, killick (anchor made of wood and stone), knees, knuckles, king devil, kelp, keepsake (charm bracelet), khaki

Ll   lobster traps, lemonade, lunch, loon, lupines, linen, lemons, Louisbourg lighthouse

Mm   moon shell, matches, meal, mates, maple leaf, Mackinaw blanket, melon, moss, mug

Nn   Newfoundland dog, naval vessel, naval officer, nighthawk, nightshade, nose (on the dog), new moon, navy blue

Oo   otter, osprey, open cave, ocean, one, Old English sheepdog, owl, overlook, orange

Pp   prow, protected cove, porpoise pod, plumage, periwinkles, peak, people, pole, puddle, purple

Qq   quilt, quarter, quahog, quay, Queen Anne's lace, *The Quoddy Tides*

Rr   rope, rubber rafts, rocks, raccoon, river, ribbon, raven, Nova Scotia duck-tolling retriever, red

Ss   sloop, spinnaker, salt water, seaboard, sunlight, sails, song sparrow, schnauzer, sundew (plant), shell, strawberries, schooner, stick, sky, sea green

Tt   Titanic, tour, truck, telegraph, ten (10), tablecloth, tableware, tines, topcoat, text, teenager, timepiece, tan

Uu   umbrella, sea urchin, underwater, upside down, undulating grass

Vv   vessels, visage, view, visitor, vine, vapor, vegetables, verdant vegetation

Ww   water, water lily, woodpecker, woods, wing, willow, wilderness, woodchuck, wood duck, wading bird, white

Xx   St. F. X. (University), X ring, treasure map "X," X-shape

Yy   yawl, yarn, yardarm, yachtsmen, youngster, New York Lady, yellow

Zz   zigzagging windsurfers: Zach, Zeus, Zenia, and Zeph; Z-shape, zeros

A Angus and Anna hope to catch trout or salmon from a flat-bottomed rowboat. Maine's rivers are among the few that support natural runs of Atlantic salmon. Deep-sea fishermen, however, may haul in swordfish, shark, or bluefin tuna.

B During the 19th century, fishing schooners sailed swiftly to and from the Grand Banks. The schooner *Bluenose*, launched in 1921 at Lunenburg, Nova Scotia, was a commercial fishing vessel and a racer that won the International Fishermen's Trophy several times. *Bluenose II*, a replica launched in 1963, represents Nova Scotia as a sailing goodwill ambassador. Many stories are told regarding the origin of the name *Bluenose*. Schooner sailors from Atlantic Canada, who exported blue potatoes with big bumps on them that looked like noses, were called Bluenoses. Greeting the majestic vessel, the people of New England cried out, "Here come the Bluenoses." It's also been said that when fishermen wiped the drips from their noses with their woolen mittens, the blue dye smudged off making their noses blue. Even today, Nova Scotians are often referred to as "Bluenoses," or more commonly, "Bluenosers."

C Cape Islanders are stable and efficient fishing boats; they can travel several miles off the coast. Depending on the time of year, the license, and the type of fishing gear used, inshore fishermen may catch crab, lobster, scallops, shrimp, turbot, mackerel, haddock, capelin, or pollock.

D Atlantic white-sided dolphins are sociable and fun-loving toothed whales. They often leap and roll through the bow wave of a boat, revealing yellowish sides and white bellies. Communicating with pilot and humpback whales, they bark, groan, chirp, whistle, and slap their flukes on the water.

E The bald eagle, the American national emblem, is easily recognized by its huge yellow bill and white tail, neck, and head. Building enormous nests in trees, bald eagles rear one or two eaglets per year. Mainly fish-eaters, they fly over water searching for prey, or steal from other birds. Bald eagles take off with deep strokes, lifting themselves higher and higher and, on flattened wings, soar through the sky. From a height of about 40 meters, or 44 yards, bald eagles can spot an object as small as a dime.

F Fossils are the hardened remains of plants and animals that have been preserved in the earth's crust. Fundy fossils include trees, plants, insects, and dinosaurs. Fossilized trees were still alive when buried, and you can see them standing upright embedded in sandstone cliffs. Massive tides carve small islands called flowerpots into the soft red sandstone. At low tide, be alert when wandering around the eroded bases of "flowerpots." The returning tide waits for no one.

G Grass and plants are essential for the preservation and control of sand dunes. Tall long-rooted marram grass anchors sand, and provides shelter for other shore plants, enabling them to take root in the dunes. Otherwise, blowing sand, dried by land and sea breezes, can bury valuable farmland, or clog fishing harbors. Did Anne Shirley run barefoot through sand dunes?

H Breaching humpback whales are acrobatic, lifting their bodies straight into the air. They can use their long flippers to stroke other whales or to wallop waves, creating loud splashing noises called flippering. Before diving, they flip their tail flukes in a kind of wave. Black-and-white markings on their tails are used to identify these whales as no two tails are the same. It's been said that male humpbacks sing the most complicated songs of the animal kingdom.

I During early summer, you can often see icebergs off the coast of Newfoundland. They have become detached from the parent glacier by a process known as calving, and drift south from Greenland and the Arctic. Entering the warm Gulf Stream, the icebergs begin to break up and melt. Spreading out in all directions, these drifting icebergs may get trapped near shore. It is exciting to find an iceberg in a coastal cove!

J Joe Batt's Arm is an authentic outport community that relies heavily on the sea to survive. There you can jig with a weighted hook on a long line that you jerk up and down over the side of a boat. Jellyfish drift into coves like this one and may be found washed up along the shorelines, tangled in seaweed. Jellyfish have saclike bodies shaped like umbrellas, with long tentacles containing stinging cells used to capture food. If you touch a dead jellyfish – watch out! Its tentacles can still sting.

K Kejimkujik is a national park best visited by canoe or kayak. Using a double-bladed paddle, kayakers glide silently through its waters observing wildlife.

L The first lighthouses to guide mariners around coastal waters were blazing bonfires, or tar burning on stakes. In 1716, Boston Light on Little Brewster Island generated one of the first beams of light from an enclosed lighthouse in the Atlantic region. In 1734, a circular stone tower at Louisbourg was the site of Canada's first lighthouse. Lighthouses, as we've known them, are now being replaced by automated metal towers.

M Blue mussels have pear-shaped shells hinged together by sturdy ligaments and muscles. Mussels fasten themselves to rocks, or to one another, by tough threadlike fibers called byssuses. You can find them in dense beds along rocky coastlines, or clumped together on wharf pilings. Because mussels are filter feeders, their flesh is easily poisoned by polluted water. Mariners say to eat mussels only in a month with the letter *R* in its name.

N Harbors are meant to be safe havens. Halifax Harbour, home to Canada's navy, is 19 kilometers, or 12 miles, in length. The Harbour narrows down, then opens up into the Bedford Basin. During World War I, convoys of ships loaded with supplies gathered in Bedford Basin to wait for an escort to Europe. On Dec. 6, 1917 a French ship, *Mont Blanc*, carrying a cargo of explosives, entered the Harbour planning to join a convoy to Europe. At the same time, a Norwegian vessel, *Imo*, was leaving the Basin heading for New York. The ships collided in The Narrows, resulting in the world's largest man-made explosion before the atomic age.

O Waves pounding the near vertical slate cliffs of Nova Scotia's south shore wore away the bluish-gray slate, forming sea caves called ovens. Many of the caves can be explored by land, or from the sea. Although the caves are natural, some were extended during the 1861 gold rush. Gold, from glacial debris and trapped in the slate, broke away from the cliffs and washed onto the shore close to The Ovens. It's been said that more gold was mined in Nova Scotia than in all of the Klondike.

P After spending the winter at sea, millions of seabirds like puffins, murres, and gannets return to the same rocky islands and cliffs to breed year after year. They eat their own weight in food every day. Guano, a natural fertilizer excreted by seabirds, is packed with nitrates and phosphates. When the cold Labrador Current meets the warm waters of the Gulf Stream, the movement fills the water with oxygen. Nutrients rise to the surface, where they are exposed to sun and oxygen, creating a nourishing soup to feed plankton. Large numbers of herring and capelin eat plankton; bigger fish like cod eat herring and capelin; and cod are eaten by seals.

Q The movement of strong currents and high tides in Passamaquoddy Bay keeps plankton living near the surface of the shallow water, attracting millions of young herring (sardines). During the late 1800s, sardines were scooped from weirs (fencelike fish traps) and carried to canneries in sloop-rigged quoddy boats, or pinkies. Fickle winds and currents often made the trip difficult. Quoddy boats were eventually put out of service by boats with more reliable gasoline-fired engines.

R The highest tides in the world occur in the Bay of Fundy. Incoming tides get squeezed by the Bay's funnel shape, causing the water to rise up and over the outgoing river flow. This creates a fast moving wave called a tidal bore that reverses the flow of some rivers (like the Shubenacadie) emptying into the Bay. When the water rushes backward into the rivers, it is possible to go white-water rafting, upriver. Mi'kmaq legends tell of the great Chief Glooscap, who controlled the tides with his magic.

S Jutting out into the Atlantic Ocean, Newfoundland's Cape Spear is North America's most easterly point (excluding Greenland). Standing by the lighthouse on its rugged cliffs, you are closer to Ireland than to Winnipeg or Miami. West Quoddy Head, Maine is the most easterly point in the continental United States.

T Tides are the regular rise and fall of ocean waters caused by the gravitational pull of the moon and sun. Twice a day ocean waters flow away from the shore, causing a "low tide." When the ocean waters return to the shore, we call it "high tide." Following the sinking of the luxury liner *Titanic* in 1912, a deck chair was found drifting toward shore, becoming one of the most popular items on display at the Maritime Museum of the Atlantic in Halifax.

U As waves crash on the beach, water from preceding waves is draining back into the sea. Standing on a sandy beach with water lapping around your ankles, you can feel the sand wash out from under your feet. Currents and tides cause this pull, which is more powerful on deeply slanted beaches. Be alert when swimming in the ocean. Remember what happened to Ursula!

V Viking sagas of voyages to Vinland inspired Norwegian explorer Dr. Helge Ingstad and his wife, Anne Stine, to organize archaeological expeditions to L'Anse aux Meadows, Newfoundland. After finding handmade iron nails, a bronze ring-headed pin, a soapstone spindle whorl, sewing tools, and broken wood objects, scientists concluded the site had been a Viking community, but probably not Vinland. UNESCO (United Nations Educational Scientific Cultural Organization) recognized the importance of the discovery by declaring L'Anse aux Meadows a World Heritage Site in 1978.

W Wetlands – like swamps, ponds, marshes, and estuaries – are natural habitats for plants, animals, fish, birds, and insects. The roots of wetland plants filter fertilizers and pollution out of the groundwater, and trap sediment that could suffocate fish. Because wetlands were often viewed as wastelands, many were filled in and developed. As a result, several plant and animal species were lost. Now that we understand the vital role of wetlands in the environment, people are working to preserve them.

X Not all treasure seekers are as lucky as Xavier. For two centuries, experts have been baffled – where is the treasure? Is it on Jewell Island, Maine, or Oak Island, Nova Scotia? Did Captain Kidd really bury treasure here, or is it just a myth?

Y British colonists who settled in Maine built one of the first ocean-going sailing vessels in North America. They named her *Virginia* and gave up their shirts for the sails. When sailing ships were no longer used for fishing and trading, sailing (or yachting) continued as a sport. One famous yachtsman, Joshua Slocum, sailed solo around the world, leaving Massachusetts in 1895 and returning in 1898. When the going got tough, he re-rigged his sloop, the *Spray*, into a yawl for easier sailing.

Z Lazy, hazy, crazy days of windsurfing can be thrilling. Exploring by water is the perfect way to observe coastlines. By investigating every bay and point along the Atlantic coast, your expedition can take you almost as far as going around the world.

Acknowledgments

The author and illustrator would like to thank the Honourable Wilfred P. Moore, Q.C., Chairman, Bluenose II Preservation Trust.
Schooner *Bluenose II* © Bluenose II Preservation Trust. Used with permission. All rights reserved.

Anne of Green Gables and *Anne Shirley* are trademarks and Canadian official marks of the Anne of Green Gables Licensing Authority Inc., which is owned by
the heirs of L. M. Montgomery and the Province of Prince Edward Island, located in Charlottetown, P.E.I. and are used under licence by Donna Grassby and Tundra Books.

The illustrator acknowledges the support of the Nova Scotia Arts Council / Conseil des arts de la Nouvelle-Écosse.

The author would like to thank: Kathy Lowinger, Sue Tate, Susan Tooke, Gerry Grassby, Marcella H. Shields, Peter Carver, Jerry Giorno,
Andrew Hebda, Ralph Getson, Heather A. Getson, Allan Doyle, Ed Kirby, David Walker, and Gordon Fader.

Locations of Illustrations

A	Bay of Fundy, Sackville, New Brunswick
B	Boston, Massachusetts
C	Indian Harbour, Nova Scotia
D	Acadia National Park, Mount Desert Island, Maine
E	Englishtown, Cape Breton, Nova Scotia
F	Hopewell Rocks at Hopewell Cape, New Brunswick
G	Cavendish Beach, Prince Edward Island
H	Witless Bay, Newfoundland
I	Merritt's Harbour, New World Island, Newfoundland
J	Joe Batt's Arm, Fogo Island, Newfoundland
K	Seaside Adjunct, Kejimkujik National Park, Nova Scotia
L	Louisbourg, Cape Breton, Nova Scotia
M	Martinique Beach, Nova Scotia
N	Halifax, Nova Scotia
O	The Ovens, Nova Scotia
P	Witless Bay, Newfoundland
Q	Eastport, Maine
R	Shubenacadie River, Maitland, Nova Scotia
S	Cape Spear, Newfoundland
T	Maritime Museum of the Atlantic, Halifax, Nova Scotia
U	Lawrencetown Beach, Nova Scotia
V	L'Anse aux Meadows National Historic Site, Newfoundland
W	Port Joli, Nova Scotia
X	Jewell Island, Maine
Y	Yarmouth, Nova Scotia
Z	Back Bay, Portland, Maine

Text copyright © 2000 by Donna Grassby
Illustrations copyright © 2000 by Susan Tooke

Published in Canada by Tundra Books, *McClelland & Stewart Young Readers*,
481 University Avenue, Toronto, Ontario M5G 2E9

Published in the United States by Tundra Books of Northern New York,
P.O. Box 1030, Plattsburgh, New York 12901

Library of Congress Catalog Number: 99-75642

Canadian Cataloguing in Publication Data

Grassby, Donna,
  A seaside alphabet

ISBN 0-88776-516-5

1. English language – Alphabet – Juvenile literature. 2. Atlantic Coast (Canada) – Pictorial works – Juvenile literature. 3. Atlantic Coast (U.S.) – Pictorial works – Juvenile literature. I. Tooke, Susan. II. Title.

PE1155.G72 2000   j421'.1   C99-932190-0

We acknowledge the support of the Canada Council for the Arts and the Ontario Arts Council for our publishing program.

We acknowledge the financial support of the Government of Canada through the Book Publishing Industry Development Program for our publishing activities.

Printed and bound in Hong Kong, China

1 2 3 4 5 6   05 04 03 02 01 00